# THE
# HELPER'S NOTES:
*Volume Two*

———

Author: D. Alt

Co-Author: Benjamin A.J.A.

**Gotham Books**

30 N Gould St.
Ste. 20820, Sheridan, WY 82801
https://gothambooksinc.com/

Phone: 1 (307) 464-7800

© 2024 *D. Alt*. All rights reserved.

No part of this book may be reproduced, stored in a retrieval system, or transmitted by any means without the written permission of the author.

Published by Gotham Books (September 20, 2024)

ISBN: 979-8-3304-2002-5 (P)
ISBN: 979-8-3304-2014-8 (E)

Because of the dynamic nature of the Internet, any web addresses or links contained in this book may have changed since publication and may no longer be valid.

The views expressed in this work are solely those of the author and do not necessarily reflect the views of the publisher, and the publisher hereby disclaims any responsibility for them.

# FOREWORD

Written by: Benjamin A.J.A.

Love mine; admire His.
Soon you won't be or act in haste as life's fruits unfold.
Do not accept another person's pressure.
He is just, just as you want it to be.
Study, meeting attendance and prayer.
Do not be overly excited when you have a plan,
or when you have money.
If you're too fast the crash will be harder,
the faster you go the harder the crash.
Our survival depends on our obedience.
Do not be afraid to take on your own responsibilities.
Do not be afraid to save your money.
Change your friends to those who will help you focus
on becoming a better you.

# DEDICATION

This book has been written to help, to assist, to heal, to uplift, and to open the hearts and minds of my readers and is therefore dedicated to you the reader.

Also, to my beautiful little Angel:

**Aaliyah Alt**

**You are loved and greatly appreciated.**

# PREFACE

I started writing this book somewhere around 2024 with the intention of baring my soul, expressing my heart, and sharing my mind for so to leave behind my legacy. It quickly became something of far greater potential as I filled page after page with inspirational quotes, motivational phrases, words of wisdom, and loving notes. The original version of the book was hand written in part, and transferred to typed.

I truly believe in the content of this book and hope that as you, the reader read and interpret what you read in your very own way that you can apply what you learn into your life somehow and that you grow from the experience of reading these pages.

It also is my hopes that you share what you have learned with your friends and family so as one we grow together. It is love & light I send you.

*He who is wise, knows knowledge is everywhere.*

# INTRODUCTION

I personally wouldn't label this a self-help book so to speak. This book is more to remind you what you are, to inspire you, and to guide you along your journey. It is not persuasive or manipulative in its way. It states simple basic fundamental truths to awaken the inner you and open the heart and mind. One who is receptive and open to incoming information is more apt to grow, and to live more prosperously than the opposite of that would be.

**You, are Loved.**

**If you want to be wise read a book an old man wrote.**

Sort your friends and know your enemies.

**Preach what you practice.**

Everything I did, I did on purpose and intentionally.

**Life will be as good as we make it to be.**

Yes you are.

**You're never finished.**

You should look at everyone with compassion.

**I think you should care about life.**

What do you want from life?

**I want to make the world a better place.**

Some people forget that love is righteous.

**If you're good you're great.**

When you were a kid what did you want to be?

**Never give up on your dreams.**

Surround yourself wisely.

**Protect what you care about.**

If you never believed in it, it would never become.

**If you believe you can, I know you will.**

Value friendship.

**I'm trying to help you.**

Nobody is standing in anyone else's shoes.

**Life can be good for you if you make the right choices.**

Care about your bonds.

**Invest in community.**

If you want to do something good,
do it one million times.

**I put my life in these pages.**

An evil person might laugh at you,
but a good person will laugh with you.

**If you want things to change
you have to do something different.**

Put good things in your mind.

**Thoughts are powerful.**

Don't be afraid to fight for what you believe in.

**Find something you care about and love
it like it's all you got.**

You make the world a better place.

**Any man's anger will prove him foolish soon enough.**

Anger doesn't solve many problems.

**Lead way compassionately.**

Some people you meet are not your friends.

**Some people don't love you like you love them.**

Some people are evil and know they're evil
but they won't tell you that.

**Study your associations.**

Pay close attention to the outcomes of your interactions
with others.

**Let no one provoke your motions.**

Try to be happy.

**Remember the good things.**

Always wish well for others.

**Satan doesn't trouble his friends.**

Just do the best you can.

**Everyone has different struggles.**

Everything you experience affects who you become.

**Value the moments and cherish the memories.**

Be careful. Don't fall in love with the wrong things.

**Don't let bad habits become you.**

You are what you continuously do.

**Don't let patience become procrastination.**

Give this world your heart not your hate.

**Change always becomes us.**

Happiness is an inside job.
It doesn't depend on things without you.

**It will never be all right but that's okay.**

Bound by word, I wrap it around you.

**Conserve your resources.**

Use your time wisely.

**Productivity depends on efficiency.**

Don't throw away good things.

**Give someone a compliment every day.**

Become true love always.

**Respect for accolade or achievement is earned.
Respect for life is given.**

I think my work within you is too great to be lost
or ignored.

**How can humanity grow and prosper?
By caring about one another.**

Drop your ego and pick up your concern for each other.

**We can accomplish more together.**

I will give until nothing's left of me.

**When troubled moments occur, best is to remain calm.**

Let your struggle serve to make you stronger.

**Be patient, kind, caring, and considerate.**

Put beautiful thoughts in your mind.

**If you're tired then rest.
You don't have to do everything right now.**

Life is meant to be lived.

**I think the journey is more important than the destination.**

You learn a lot as you grow and age.

**True leaders leave the class last.**

Don't judge yourself for your own mistakes
but use them to grow.

**I can't solve everyone's problems.**

No matter how much I care about people, they were blessed with free will and their choices are their decisions.

**Avoid people who intentionally lie a lot.**

I'm not here to hurt this world,
I'm here to help and inspire it.

**The psychic spirit promotes sickness and death.
They are scattered amongst you.**

Demons are not gargoyles.

**You can't change what you can't change.**

Men will be men and boys will be boys.

**Focus on being positive mentally
because what you think you will become.**

Sometimes you have to fight your way to a better life.

**Make sure you have a good day.**

Before you rest each night take a moment to make peace with yourself knowing that you did the best that you could.

**There's two truths and one is a lie.**

Some people hide behind their own faces.

**Hate is deceptive. Love is so transparent that it will risk humiliation if it has to.**

Before I die, I will change this world.

**Some people don't want to see you happy.**

The world will drain you if you let it.

**My life is a love song.**

Invest in communion.

**God will use humility to humble you.**

It's 3:10 AM March 14$^{th}$ 2024 and I am still up, and still working, and still writing this book to motivate and inspire you all.

**Only Jesus loves you more than I do.**

I carry the cross.

**Wake your light up.**

What you think, your body believes.

**Stress and worry can weaken the immune system and cause physical sickness.**

Think good thoughts and be positive.

**A friend of a friend is my friend too.**

Embrace the truth, avoid the lie,
and know the difference between the two.

**Try to see the positive or good in things.**

Be optimistic.

**Inspire a positive evolution.**

Find your way but enjoy the journey.

**Everything will serve a purpose.**

If you work to enhance goodness in the world
then the world will change.

**Care should always be there.**

Change is a constant.

**Try not to let worldly wounds hurt your heart.
There's always a way.**

I care about you,
and I have consideration for what you're going through.

**Hatred is too hard to hold.**

Just be kind to one another.

**My words are my gift to you.**

Stay strong.

**Promote unity.**

Happiness is the purest form of energy you will ever find.
The reason why is because emotion is spiritual
and affects the soul.

**Stress and depression create negative physical effects.**

I fought the world for you and won.

**Hope is something you should always hold.**

When life seems hectic or even chaotic at times important
is to remain calm and hold inner peace so you can make
the right decisions.

**You're stronger than the storm.**

Let the light of your love and care bless the life
that we all live and share.

**My life is self-sacrifice.**

I'm going through a lot but still helping you.

**Appreciate the good things about yourself and others.**

Never give up on yourself.

**You are love I remind you.**

Value your bonds.

**Don't let this world corrupt you.**

Sometimes the world can be cruel and cold, stay strong and maintain and don't let this world spoil your heart.

**You are you.**

Too much power could corrupt almost any man.

**I inject my word into the spirit of life.**

Some humor is good and some humor is not.
It depends on how good or bad you are.

**I think men think about war too much.**

You can only be young once.

**You better care about something.**

I'm the champion of my heart.

**I believe in good things.**

Sometimes I think ants have more respect for each other than people do.

**My truth is one to live by.**

Be a good friend.

**Don't look at people the wrong way.**

Be humble and be calm but don't be afraid to let right clash with wrong.

**Find someone who will love you through it all and stay with you forever.**

No one wants to be lonely.

**If you focus on the quality of your work then when you place your work, your work will inspire and be remembered by everyone who sees it.**

Be consistent but patient with the process.

**If you don't try your best doing what you do then you're wasting your time.**

Like a candle in the night, I give you light.

**Don't rush things but take your time.**

Don't let this world tell you
that you can't be what you want to be.

**Never sacrifice your integrity.**

Invest in your output.

**You were made for a reason and planned for a purpose.
Give this world the best of you.**

Protect the quality of your character.

**Everything takes time.**

Shame to ones who deceive another.

**Stop worrying, it's going to be okay.**

This life we live is not a game.

**Life is not a scrimmage.**

If you died right now, would you be happy with your life?

**Education is vital to our survival.**

Everybody starts somewhere.

**Love them like I love you.**

Persevere.

**Life is not a privilege; life is an obligation.**

Open the blinds, let some sunshine in.

**Affect the world for the better.**

Practice positive influence.

**Focus on what you can do or can change.**

Always believe in you.

**Give life to the love in your heart.**

Do not be afraid.

**We are all in process of becoming.**

I want to affect your life.

**Better is the effect of love.**

No one's life is easy.

**I will touch your heart and open your mind.**

Fast is the pace of a race, slow is the walk.

**Everyone affects life in some way or another. Make sure your effect adds up.**

Don't let a bad day spoil a good life.

**Never be afraid to be you.**

Hug yourself for me.

**I believe that my words can change your perspective if you give the time to read them.**

I wrote and I wrote and I wrote.

**Be time wise.**

Be careful what you feed your brain.

**Not everyone is as able as you.**

Do your best to in some way make a positive impact.

**In these books and in these pages,
this is what I think and believe.**

I like the evolution of love.
It will bring us all closer as friends and family.

**We're better together.**

Strive if you have to, but get where you want to be,
and achieve what you want to achieve.
You will if you keep going.

**I can't give up on you. I don't know how to do that.**

Don't give up on yourself.

**Everyday can be a good day.**

Let your love radiate positive energy.

**Develop the quality of your character.**

Never be less than good.

**Great it is that is good.**

If your heart is your vault protect your worth.

**What am I doing? Sowing and planting seeds.**

If you need a break, take a break.

**Lead by way of example and positive influence to point others in the right direction.**

Disagreements will occur. Best is to let them be just verbal and never let them become physical.

**Physical violence cannot solve verbal arguments or clashing of ideas.**

Avoid anger. It clutters, frustrates, and confuses the mind and becomes a terrible energy to hold.

**Your mind, body, and soul are intertwined as one to form one and each individual.**

I believe the world can be a better place.

**The world doesn't need more weapons. It needs more hearts and extended hands.**

If you want to be strong, be love.

**Here's a secret: The soul rules the body but the mind tells the soul what to do.**

A happy soul is a healthy soul.

**Just be the love you are.**

To ants we are giants but to the universe we are ants.

**The world doesn't value life enough.**

Hate is harsh and ugly but love is a beautiful thing.

**Let time fortify your bonds.**

Trust is difficult to regain after its broken.

**Establish and protect the history of your character by always doing or striving to do the right things.**

In basketball if you want to score 100 points shoot 1,000 times.

**Be considerate.**

Protect your peace.

**Tomorrow is another day and another chance to try.**

Tomorrow is another chance at life.

**Man's quest for power could destroy him.**

Life is a place that we all belong.

**Caring is how this works.**

Grow at your own pace.

**There's something special about my pages.**

Can you hear my battle cry?

**My word is my sword.**

Sacrifice your wants for your needs.

**Before go to war or engage in physical conflict, ask yourself, is there any other way.**

Train yourself to be righteous.

**I'm writing you love letters.**

Maintain a calm demeanor.

**Even if chaos is all around you, you must remain calm to ensure you make the right choices and decisions.**

It's not the speed of the pace but the quality of the effort that defines results.

**I think my books are the best way I can reach you.**

If you're willing to learn you're willing to grow.

**Always be willing to grow.**

Good is the honor of brave men.

**Noble is the quality of a good man.**

I will fight the life you live with all of me and wrap my word around it.

**Today is Sunday, March 17th 2024. It is 2.22 AM.**
**I am still up, still working, and still writing.**
**I will change the world.**

I know who I am and I know that my word can change the world. I write and I write and I right.

**At the least don't hurt or destroy anything.**

I will not stop. I will not quit.

**Invest in your future not your past.**

Like water is my word because my word is the truth.
If you read it you will grow.

**My pain is beautiful.**

Only peace within us all can create peace around us all.

**I try to make better everywhere I go before leaving.
I don't want to damage life.**

Don't let the world corrupt your heart.

**We all need peace not war.**

Because we battle the spirit and not the flesh
we're all at war with ourselves.

**Everyone should try to try on another person's shoes.
Everyone should try to see another person's perspective.
That would enhance the consideration and compassion
we have for each other.**

You are you and I am I but together we are.

**Sometimes I use music to drowned my demons.
I must keep going and cannot let them stop me.**

My words could heal the world.

**Make anything against you make you stronger.**

Live a truthful life.

**A weapon in the right hand is a form of protection.
A weapon in the wrong hand is a threat to society.**

This is my life and this is what I know.

**You can learn a lot from a silent man.**

You owe no explanations.

**My word is my flesh.**

Avoid excessive motions.

**Strive to do the right things and fight your life forward with goodness.**

Love yourself.

**Be courageous.**

Tell yourself positive things.

**You're not the only one struggling.**

Lend a hand sometimes.

**Take care of yourself and those you love.**

Work towards your goals.

**Become unbothered.**

Don't dwell on your problems so much
but think about and ponder solutions.

**I think you should read for at least thirty minutes or an hour every day. It helps to open the mind when we share perspectives.**

My goal is to inspire you.

**Not everyone is worthy of your time.**

Sometimes your enemies will deceive you with the friendliest faces.

**I believe that until we all drop our pride and drop our search for power the world will be a harsh place.
Guard your heart.**

Separate your wants from your needs and know
the difference.

**Save some money for rainy days.**

Express your personality.

**If it's not hurting you, you should not attack it.**

Try not to waste anything, especially your money.

**Practice patience.**

You're as strong as you want to be.

**Every one of you has positive potential.**

Hope for good things.

**Don't let money influence your motives.**

Better is to move in silence than to announce your every motion. When you announce your every motion, you're teaching your enemy the devil how to tamper with your goals.

**The devil will steal your joy if you let him.**

Even insects have an opinion.

**Respect life.**

If you fail to respect life you will in somehow and someway be punished.

**Then is then and now is now.**

You cannot destroy your past but you can work towards making your future better.

**Be responsible and hold yourself accountable.**

Sometimes you don't get a second chance.

**You should always want to do what's right.**

Conquer yourself, not the world.

**If you inspire people, it will naturally motivate them.**

Lead by providing proper example.

**There's a way this all works.**

Care about what you care about.

**Everyone's battling something.**

It takes of us all to create peace.

**You will find what you're searching for.**

If you love it, you will give it your time.

**I'd give the world a hug if I could.**

I think the world needs more hugs and tears.

**Before you get to the cheers you get more pains, disappointments, and tears but you must persevere.**

Beware of poker faces.

**Some days will make you happy,
Some days will make you sad,
But every day will make you grow.**

Don't let the world confuse you. Good is good, Bad is bad, right is right, and wrong is wrong.

**Avoid pessimists.**

Sometimes you will struggle but when you overcome that struggle you will be stronger.

**Defeat yourself.**

Care about the broken hearted.

**Raindrops keep falling on my rooftop.**

My truth is the truth that is forever.

**Enhance weakness; Announce it as strength.**

I'm exercising your mind.

**Some lessons are not easy to learn.**

Life was impossible without pain.

**Tell them all I love them.**

The only way you will get through this is together.

**Give to the needy when you can.**

If it doesn't help it hurts.

**Raise these generations.**

True love is unending.

**If we all give the world our heart the world will become our love.**

Dedicate yourself to the right things.

**Make responsible choices and decisions.**

Your neighbor is not your enemy.

**Always be a helping hand.**

Even a bug's life matters.

**Choice is inevitable but challenge is an option.
You can stay the same or grow.**

You are one of many.

**I am the lighthouse.**

Thank you, Nostradamus.

**You can't make other people's choices for them,
but you can inspire them though.**

Don't let your fear become a giant.

**Don't waste your own time worrying.**

You are special and you are unique.

**Approach life with positive energy.**

From mind fades to flesh.

**Together we battle the spirit of evil.**

If you want to know it enough, you'll learn it.

**Never be careless.**

Don't rush your works.

**Sometimes you have to create your own sunshine.**

The greatest gift you can give is a smile.

**Appreciate those who treated you kindly.**

Life is as big as you perceive it to be.

**Be calm when opinions clash.**

Give the world nothing less than your best.

**Sometimes you have to ignore the nonsense.**

You don't want to be at the mercy of man.

**Don't let other people control your time.**

Protect your innocence.

**Maintain your rightward walk.**

Be consistent.

**My tongue is sharper than your sword.**

Don't kill it unless you're going to eat it.

**Grass is not a living thing. It does not have an opinion or freedom of motion and is held in cycle by photosynthesis.**

Just because something continues
and it develops does not mean it's a living thing.

**Cars rust. Are those living things?**

To be living you must have an opinion.

**Be slowly spoken and fast to forgive.**

Being fast to forgive is being slow to anger.

**Be not ill minded. If you are ill minded
your own wickedness will consume you.**

Be cautious of what contradicts your will.

**Live your life how you want to, and live by your own terms.**

Strive through struggle, endure through pain,
make yourself stronger,
and know that every day will not be the same.

**You can be what you want to be.**

Avoid self-destructive thoughts, patterns, and habits.

**Build yourself up.**

A good life starts with good thoughts.

**Nobody will walk your feet for you.**

Don't complain about accessories while some people are dying because they don't have necessities.

**Some people are not as able as you.**

God's children cannot eat your Ferrari.

**First things first, one step at a time.**

You need to learn how to keep each other, and stop throwing your bonds away.

**Take the bad with the good, I guess.**

Work always produces results.

**Rustle the bushes and ruffle their feathers.**

If you are good someone does not like you that's their problem not yours. Just be you.

**Every man must walk his own feet and choose his own fate.**

Destiny is reached by way of faith.

**Man's quest for power and global control could consume him and destroy us all.**

You can only do the best that you can do.

**Don't curse your effort with arrogance.**

My heart is a word to live by.

**Faith will get you further than footsteps.**

It's probably very important if I say it more than once.

**I don't pretend to be, I am really very good.**

Take from my word what you want because I know that what you take from my word is what you need.

**You're here together whether you like it or not.**

Everyone has options.

**Everyone's job is to be good.**

If you give a little, it'll pay you back a lot.

**If you care about them, tell them today.**

Tomorrow is not a promise.

**Be careful what you say, and how you talk to each other. Words are powerful.**

Bonds are not meant to be broken.

**Invest your time in good things.**

Life is precious.

**Hold your heart.**

Be careful what you let appeal to you.

**Think twice, react once.**

I think that some men are obsessed with power.
Is it because they are afraid?

**Provoke thought, not motion.**

Let every man make his own decisions.

**Don't ever touch love the wrong way.**

Don't throw yourself away.

**You are treasure and you are not trash.**

I think everyone should be a humanitarian.

**The world needs more hearts not handcuffs.**

If you care enough to reach, you can touch their hearts, open their minds, and inspire the kind of change that we all need.

**Don't hate, hate with hate, that's a negative equation, but hate, hate with love.**

You cannot control another man's choices.

**Let them make their own choices and decisions because then you will know who they truly are.**

I will give you light.

**Why am I so strong? Because I am love.**

Missiles are not stronger than handshakes.

**You are not alone, we are together.**

I won't be happy until you see my truth.

**What am I doing? Writing love letters.**

I am the love and I am the law.

**What did you do with your two hands?**

I don't want to leave the world without handing it my heart.

**Utilize your resources wisely.**

Money isn't really worth anything.

**Man will not conquer the world until he conquers himself.**

What's inside you is greater than what's around you.

**Free is what a man gives from his heart.**

Practice goodness daily.

**I'm smart enough to know I'm not a lie,
and kind enough to continue my truth.**

Many times, your enemy will disguise himself as your friend because he's a coward.

**If you ever get angry make sure it's for the right reason.**

Physical violence will not solve your verbal disputes.

**A father will make men of boys.**

My heart is a lake and my love is a river.

**Every man has an opinion.**

You can't always control what happens,
but you can control how you react to it.

**Quiet is man announcing his confidence.**

Stand affirmed.

**God's anger is righteous, man's anger is dangerous.**

We're all actually on the same team.

**You can stare at my word all day long if you want to,
but you cannot prove it to not be the truth.**

I'm the thunder in the rain, I'm the rumble in the clouds,
I am here and I am now.

**Your mother is my mother is our mother is we.**

Yield appropriately.

**The world is obsessed with war.**

Don't give up on what you believe in.

**If you are good and you know you are good then establish your presence. The world is yours.**

You're not alone, together we are.

**Sometimes a smile is the greatest gift you can give someone.**

Help each other.

**You're here together for a reason.**

Not wise is to conquer your enemies' flesh. Wise is to defeat his perspective.

**Study evolution and innovation. If you want to lead these generations you have to find unseen angles and options.**

Always be ready.

**Consider everything including your responses.**

If he is bad, kill not him as a man, but kill his ideas.

**Just be good, that's how life works.**

Play your position.

**Anchor your hopes.**

Theres so many ways to war, but only one way to love.

**Your offense should be as good as your defense
but you should rely on your defense first.**

If you want to be righteous read my word.

**Walk in consideration of all things.**

Eradicate evil.

**Be humble in victory.**

Smart is a man who accepts opportunity
but wise is a man who is prepared for it.

**You are all actually powerful.**

Think about what you can do, not what you can't do.

**Every day is another chance.**

I believe that together we can do better.

**Send hope and hugs, not missiles and rockets.**

It will take of all of us to change this life
that we all live and share together.

**If you believe what you're doing is right then keep going,
but if you believe what you're doing is wrong
then you need to stop immediately.**

There's always a right and wrong way.

**Avoid chasing pages and focus on the quality of your content.
If you're just chasing pages the quality of your content
will suffer.**

Wise men are slowly spoken.

**Write your goals down.**

The hardest part is getting it started. Once you begin and you gain momentum it gets easier to continue.

**Instead of declaring it wrong you should look at my work and see how it's true.**

I spent a lot of time thinking about you.

**Work when you have to, rest when you need to.**

My word is living water.

**Happy people make other people happy.**

Music can move the world.

**Don't be afraid to be universal.**

I put my heart in these pages

**Adjust to the times because the time won't adjust to you.**

To create a global change, you have to contradict their opinions but key to that is finding the opinion that's always right.

**I know that I have not more than I give.**

Destroy the world's perspective.

**Consume what you must and save what you need. Conserve your resources.**

This is who I am and this is what I know.

**You can't pull a man out of quicksand if you're standing in it yourself.**

I think rent should be free.

**Make everyone you meet better.**

I know everything I gain here I will lose.

**Sometimes it's necessary to unlearn
what the world teaches you.**

If you are a world leader and you want your nation to excel,
make education affordable.

**Never let your will to learn die.**

Try to always pay attention.

**Observe as much as you can.**

Try not to be lazy minded.

**No one can be you better than you.**

You learn more when you watch and listen a lot.
You don't learn when you're the one speaking.

**When you're working on things or looking at life ask as many questions as you can. That's how you learn and grow.**

If you ask the right questions you'll receive the right answers.

**Life's not supposed to be a chess match.**

You can be what you want to be.

**Don't make fun of others.**

Avoid ugly thoughts.

**Don't celebrate early. Celebrate your success when your victory has been fully achieved.**

I will only rest my work when I need to.

**Value the time other people have given you. Don't take it for granted.**

Be the love and light you are.

**You will only get through this together.**

Don't invest in stress.

**Put your mind in a positive place.**

Happiness is a strength.

**Alcohol is an amplifier not a depressant.**

I think you should care more and judge less.

**I know poor men who know more than rich men.
Be careful what you value.**

Greed is an unquenchable thirst for more.

**Some people don't know how to be human.**

I'd die writing these pages if I could.

**I think you should love what you care about.**

Face life's obstacles fearlessly.

**Find the one that loves your flaws.**

Life will never be perfect, just accept that fact.
Everyone's idea of perfect is different.

**Care about the right things.**

Inside everyone is alone.

**We need each other.**

True is true and false is false.

**This is the best way I can reach you all.**

Seek the truth as you avoid the lies.

**Some people love war but everyone needs peace.**

Beware of actors who haven't suffered for their roles.
By actors I mean liars.

**I don't trust anyone who hasn't struggled.**

Know that everyone is not the same.

**I am my gift to the world.**

Have you forgotten you're not alone?

**I put what I believe in these pages.**

Sometimes you can't just tell someone something and expect them to learn it. They have to actually go through it and learn from experience.

**Nothing can replace actual experience.**

Watch more and speak less.

**Don't announce your arrival.**

A loud man is easily targeted.

**Every time you shoot you give away your location.**

To find your purpose find something you love to do and develop it and get good at it.

**Why would you want more than you need?**

I believe that if you have the will to read it,
my word can help heal the world.

**War always leads to destruction.**

If you have to strike your enemy you should be swift
and quiet as a mouse.

**Everyone does not perceive the world the same.**

Not everyone loves like you do.

**War is suicide.**

Some people run away from danger
and some people run through it.

**How do I know so much? I'll tell you later.**

Man's obsession with power and control could easily
cause his demise.

**Almost every man thinks he owns the world he did not create.**

Never hold ill will for another.

**Always hope for good things to happen.**

Even if your situation is not so good,
still wish well for others.

**Despise wicked ways.**

You are stronger than you think you are.

**I hope you open this book every once in a while,
flip it to a random page and find exactly what you need.**

This book is not meant to be read fast or straight through.
It's meant to be read slowly and pondered.
I hope you can apply my quotes to your life somehow.

**I will touch your heart before I die
but this book isn't about me, it's about you.**

It's okay to let your mind wander sometimes,
you might find some great ideas.

**You're pondering when your mind wanders.**

By way of text, I place my work within you.

**Learn how to evolve properly.**

Retain what you know is true,
and discard what you find is false.

**Develop your own opinion based on facts and experience.**

No one else is you.

**Be careful what you feed your brain.**

Be careful what you invest your time in.

**If it's not good it's bad, if it's not true it's false,
if it's not right it's wrong.**

Some people like to do the wrong things
but that doesn't have to be you.

**I was 28 when I started the first volume of
The Helper's Notes. I am 40 now.**

Everybody wants to be something.

**Life won't always be the same for you.**

Times change and people change.

**Appreciate the moments, cherish the memories.**

Pride is a sin but to be proud is not.

**You are in control of what you think about.**

Everything evolves.

**Don't waste your time worrying.**

Build yourself up, don't tear yourself apart.

**How you choose to spend your own time is important to your growth and mental health.**

Don't be afraid to apologize if you find out
or learn that you're wrong.

**Don't approach life with negative energy.**

Sometimes we don't get what we want because
what we want is not what we need.

**Every man chooses his choices.**

If you want to do something good practice it.
If you want to do something great then practice it a lot.

**You can only better your best.**

Let your word not hurt but heal.

**You should care about every living thing.**

Don't let anybody tell you that you can't be you.
Don't let the world break your heart.

**Learn how to multiply your time and make it work for you.
Make wise investments.**

Don't keep all your money in one place.

**Try to save more than you spend.**

If you have enemies you need to gather counter intel
and know everything you can about them
and prepare for anyway, they could possibly attack you.

**Intentionally placing false information
could confuse your enemy.**

Wise is to expect everything.

**If you expect everything nothing will surprise you.**

What you don't know can hurt you.

**Some people don't have good intentions.**

At this time the world is not a safe place.

**Because time is in continuance and change is a constant, the world is always getting either better or worse.**

I think we all should value peace more.

**If man learns to love peace more than he loves war we will all be in a better place.**

Communicate your concerns.

**You need more balance in your life.**

You should love life more than death.

**It's a waste of time to argue with fools
who refuse to even try to understand your views.**

Some things you just have to do yourself.

**Today is March 23rd, 2024. My hands and feet are swollen.
I have trouble sleeping and puke almost every time I wake up.
My health is failing and I'm still helping you.**

Life was not possible without sacrifice.

**I cannot tell you how bad it is going to get,
but somehow, I know how good it could be.**

Value your works and invest only your best efforts
into this life that we all live.

**Struggle builds strength and establishes the quality of
your character.**

Never betray yourself.

**I only kill it if I have to,
or if I'm going to make it my breakfast, lunch, or dinner.**

You don't want to know how smart I am.

**Everyday I get up and fight life again.**

Manage your time right.

**We're supposed to be friends and family, not enemies.**

Life will break you if it has to, to make you.

**Put love where it needs to be most.**

Anyone can be good if they want to be.

**If you want to find the perfect job,
find what you love to do and do it better than anyone else.**

I like to help people.

**If you refuse to learn you will still be stupid.**

I have no sympathy for a man who is able
but too lazy to try.

**Think about good things.**

Avoid being selfish.

**If man cared about each other more than he cares about
power life would be a beautiful place.**

There is only one humanity.

**You can't stop what's meant to be.**

Every now and then someone comes along
and completely changes how you look at things.

**You don't have the right to force another man's motions.**

I believe any dispute can be resolved with
proper communication and understanding.

**There's a time to talk and a time to listen.**

Sometimes we all feel like that.

**Be your own sunrise.**

I think you should try to learn something every day.

**When you stop growing you begin to die.**

Love each other more than money.

**Love your friends and family and care about
and be considerate of your neighbors.**

Never abuse someone's kindness.

**Love is a feeling but it's also a choice.**

If you didn't invest your best, you wasted your time.

**To alter humanities path and create a global change
or shift of perspective it will take us all.**

Never forget how to be human.

**Let the love inside you become outside you.**

Everybody needs good news.

**Celebrate your differences.**

Don't take advantage of the care and consideration others give you.

**Notice everything but don't tell them all that you did.**

I will fight this life until it becomes the best of me.

**Don't give up on what you care about.**

If you care about the right things
then the wrong things should really anger you
but there's a proper way to contradict them.

**If you care about it enough,
you'll work and invest effort to keep it.**

A silent man is a powerful one.

**Speak rarely but listen always.**

If I really want to trick my enemy, I'll scatter his thoughts and make him play with his own mind.

**I am everything I say I am.**

Sometimes the most you can say is nothing.

**Stop judging other people.**
**You don't know what they went through to become them.**

Fall in love with something.

**Never let hate leave your voice.**

You should all be the voice of love.

**Be careful what you say with the tongue.**

Know when quiet is to be kept.

**You always learn while listening,**
**You never learn while speaking.**

Sometimes it has to rain.

**Anyone's attitude can be contagious.**

We need each other.

**Life will beat you up if it has to just to make us all better.**

You don't own life, we all do.

**I made my voice a rare occasion.**

Avoid too much of anything.

**I wish man thought about how to help each other more than they think about war.**

There's a time to work and there's a time to play.
There's a time to rest and there's a time to wake.
There's a time to remember and there's a time to reflect.

**Perfect your perspective.**

Together we can.

**No one deserves to be lonely.**

If your achievements are boasted about,
let it be from someone else.

**Teach yourself how to be right.**

If you don't know something just admit you don't know it,
but if you want to learn it invest effort.

**Bigger and badder isn't always better.**

Quiet, calm, and humble is more powerful
than most people think.

**Don't tell your enemy what to expect.**

Your voice is valuable.

**Don't announce your presence with a bang.
If you absolutely have to announce your presence,
announce it with a boom.**

One of the hardest lessons I had to learn in life
is everyone's not good.

**I've given life more than I could afford.
I will still keep giving of me until the date of my death.
I suppose that could define pain.**

Rainy days make love of sunshine.

**Try not to let petty arguments consume too much
of your time.**

Don't dwell on things that don't matter.

**Some people love peace and some people love war.**

Don't waste your time arguing with someone who won't
even try to consider your opinions or point of view.

**You don't always have to prove your point to others.
Sometimes it's pointless.**

My hope is for you and not against you.

**My way of dealing with physical pain is to consider it a modified version of myself. I adapt to it.**

It's wise to be happy.

**Everyone don't see everything the same way.**

Sometimes you just need to put the headphones on and blast your favorite song.

**Of my word I say:
take what you want and keep what you need.**

You can inspire to motivate the change within others but you can't control another person's choices and actions.

**Everybody needs somebody sometimes.**

Spend a little time alone.

**Love only abandons hate.**

There's always two ways to see one thing.

**Your thoughts will invade your flesh.**

Be humble but be strong, be passive but aggressive.

**Never prey on the weak, protect the meek.**

Don't let money conquer your conscious.
Money's only worth something
because the next man said it is.

**Be careful what you value.**

Always use your strength for the right reason.
You shouldn't want to be stronger than you need to be.

**Never let people around you be more than your third eye can see.**

If you find a snake, cut the whole house down.

**Solve your problems fast and swiftly.**

Silence is to be mastered.

**What you know is worth a lot, what you have is worthless.**

Enjoy your time as much as you can.

**Things won't always be this bad.**

Things won't always be this good.

**Try to go about everything rightly.**

Everyone needs rest sometimes.

**I think humanity pins itself against each other because its afraid and it don't see really were all supposed to be on the same team.**

We all share this life.

**If you want to deceive your enemy feed him false information.**

Life is too short to worry about other people's problems.

**Some people are not good and they intentionally impose their problems on you to trouble you and consume your time.**

Be good until the last day.

**Care about yourself, but care about others too.**

You cannot control life.

**Find something you care about.**

Every man has a purpose.

**Expect my silence.**

If you have enough power to start a war,
you have enough power to stop a war.

**What you care about the most will eventually emerge.**

Avoid people who play psychological games.

**Never lie to someone that you owe the truth to.**

Love should lead with concern, consideration,
compassion, and empathy for one another.

**Everything made is with reason.**

Always be appropriate.

**Sometimes hurt people hurt people.**

Broken hearts can be healed.

**Avoid bad habits.**

The best way to stop a bad habit is never to start one.

**We have to raise these generations.**

I placed my word on earth.

**What is seen by the eye will at times be tried.**

I believe that everyone knows how to love, and I believe that if you think you don't, you still can learn how.

**Never give up on yourself.**

Don't even kill a bug.

**Everything placed was on purpose.**

God is good.

**I guess we live and we learn.**

Sometimes the closest people to you hate you the most.

**Form an understanding with life.**

You should become my heart.

**Where there's fire there's flare.**

I think men like to destroy each other.

**You don't always have to reply.**

Look at the right things.

**To go to hell is easy.**

Good does get angry sometimes.

**You have to accept that you can't control
other people's choices.**

Never miss an opportunity of love.
By caring about each other the life gets better.

**I'm crazy about what I care about.**

Protect your responsibilities.

**Achieve your abilities.**

Look at your mind like a muscle,
you need to exercise that too.

**The mind is too powerful to waste.**

What you think you will become, because thought fades
to flesh. I'll tell you why, and how I know this later.
My word became flesh.

**God's temper is not your toy.**

Focus less on what you want and more on what you need.

**Sex is actually a sin, which is why Jesus Christ came here
by way of a virgin.**

Jesus's Father technically cannot sin because he is the
source of all things and everything that sinned,
has sinned against him.

**I'm still watching you watch me.**

You never have the right to be angry at God.

**Don't ever say hate is who I am.**

You can't save them all.

**Some people are victims of their own choices and decisions.**

Never abuse knowledge.

**If you want to surprise your enemy down play your ability.**

Never tell your enemy you can do more than you can do. Always tell them less of you because in doing so you create an advantage for you.

**Nothing can replace time.**

If you want to confuse your enemy then intentionally place false information but make sure you are more powerful than the information you place.

**The world is not at peace, the world is at war.**

You don't owe the world at war the truth.
You owe the world at war whatever it is that will ensure goodness survives.

**Some say that there's no honor amongst thieves.
I think they lied.**

Sometimes it gets cold.

**Tell them your secrets later.**

If you are lying to me while I'm telling you the truth,
who's right and who's wrong, me or you?

**Fall in love with beautiful thoughts.**

The truth is a powerful thing.

**Make today a good day.**

You're dealing with a few things: good and bad, right and wrong and true and false. Let that guide your decisions.

**The soul rules the body but the mind rules the soul.**

Guard your heart and protect your peace.

**In your heart make it so it is that care is always there.**

You don't have permission to hate each other.

**I'm kind of like a cramp.
The only way to conquer me is to endure me.**

I never hated what I held in my hand and hold in my heart. That's my way of saying I love what I care about.

**Try to be content.**

Doing what's right isn't always easy.
Do what's right anyway.

**Perfect your ideas.**

Rest your work sometimes and take breaks when you need to.

**Avoid people who make other people's lives harder.**

Learn how to detach yourself from everything that is draining your energy or changing you for worse.

**Don't let the world define you.**

Keep doing what you know is right.

**Don't worry about what people think of you.
Just keep doing the right things.**

Some people don't want you to be happy.
That's sad but true.

**Never laugh at or take pleasure of another person's pain.**

Be what you want to be.

**Make the world become you.**

Don't focus on your past too much.

**Yesterday prepares you for today.**

Your always either adding or subtracting.
Build yourself up don't tear yourself apart.

**Appreciate and value good things.**

Think about what you can do, and not what you can't do.
Don't ever discourage yourself.

**To be perfect is not the objective.**

Do good. Keep your hands clean.

**When someone else does not do the right things, then that's their fault and not yours.**

Train yourself to be righteous.

**Prove intention by actions.**

Care more about what you do for others more than what you do for yourself.

**Talk to him all day and every day, I promise he's there and he is very quiet.**

Prayer is petition.

**You would be afraid of me if you knew what I know.**

God is good.

**You're not your appearance.
You are what you know inside you is the truth of you.**

What you think you will become.

**Every man has his reasons.**

Everyone's a part of the plan
but some people choose to make the wrong choices.

**There's power in your heart.**

What you don't know can hurt you.

**Nurture your bonds.**

We all need each other.

**Don't flaw your friendships.**

To be good is to be great.

**Know what you need and when.**

Know what you don't need.

**Before your life here ends, try to somehow or in some way make the world a better place.**

Accept your own imperfections.

**I like to provoke thought not motion.**

If you don't believe in it, don't do it.

**Don't let anyone tell you that you cannot do, or become what you want to.**

Doing what's right should be your personal agenda.

**Be confident but avoid arrogance.**

Arrogance is a character flaw.

**Know what is your right and what is not.**

You should always be kind unless someone forces righteous anger.

**Don't let yourself do what you know is wrong.**

God is everywhere around you.

**I could conquer this world from my mother's couch.**

If you could hurt them, you could help them.

**Seek to understand all things.**

Open your heart.

**Take a break from your works sometimes.
Balance is essential.**

Life is supposed to be fun.

**I work when I want, and I sleep when I can.**

Anyone can be good.

**Sometimes your truth does not appeal to my interest.**

Make good goals.

**Do not give up when things get difficult.
Behind the scenes things are working out for your favor
and the better good of humanity.**

Bluffing is dangerous for you not them.

**It's not wise to tell them what you know or got unless you
got more than what you tell them you know or got.**

Be careful of a man who places his mistakes on purpose.

**There's something to learn from everything.**

God is teaching you both inside and out.

**What you say about them says a lot about you.**

Your motive should always be love.

**Not doing what you say you will do will cause you a loss of respect and people will stop believing you.**

Thoughts fade to flesh. Be careful about your thoughts because they could infect your flesh, which is also why stress and worry can cause physical illnesses or weaken your immune system.

**If you ask me for money, I will tell you no.
If you ask for knowledge I might tell you yes.**

The stronger the love, the weaker the hate.

**Stop telling other people all your problems.**
**Some people don't care and some people are actually glad you have those problems.**

You have to learn when to speak and when not to.
Not everyone is worthy of your voice.

**Study, study, study; read, read, read.**

You have to be wise enough to read through them and see what their real target or objective is.

**Never let no one drop your level.**

Be really good, not just for you but for others too.

**No two righteous forces have ever collided.**
**One is always right and one is always wrong.**

Share good ideas with each other.

**Spiritually happy is strong while sad becomes weak.**

Listen to good music that inspires and influences positive emotions.

**It always costs someone to give something away.**

Give graciously.

**Don't look at your neighbor as an enemy unless he has proven to be that.**

People will be who they want to be.

**You can't cage another man's thoughts.**

If you force upon another man what he can and can't do you'll never know who he truly is.

**Let them make their decisions and choices and respond accordingly.**

Ask your neighbor if you can cut their grass for free, and if they say yes then put in the work to do it.

**Never disrespect the elderly.**

The world needs more love and light,
and care and kindness.

**God punishes you for not being the love
he sent you here to be.**

Sometimes bad things happen to you because you were
not grateful and did not appreciate the good things that
you have been given.

**The quality of your work says a lot about your integrity.**

You should value doing things the right way.

**Never touch love the wrong way and always touch life
the right way.**

What you think about the most will win
within you always.

**The strongest form of the spirit is happiness.**

What are you fighting for?

**You can't always make everyone happy.**

I don't sleep much because I work a lot
but I will wake your heart up.

**Don't let your mind die inside you.**

Keep learning and keep growing.

**I think living should be simple.**

Sometimes it's hard to survive.

**Never let someone force you to sacrifice your own values
and do the wrong thing.**

You should never want too much.

**Timing does matter.**

I attacked the world with positive thoughts
and handed it my heart.

**You don't need the worlds approval.**

Just be you.

**I am always at work on myself.**

I think the dumbest thing that a person could be is racist.

**Love is colorblind.**

God made it, but no one actually owns the universe.

**You could learn a lot from each other.**

Only lie if you have to.

**No one is as strong as you.**

I wrote and wrote helping you.

**Ego is not a good thing and is not beneficial when we gather all of our ideas.**

I like logical things.

**Be open minded.**

Never disrespect the dead.

**The dead have bragging rights.**

I died to deliver my word.

**Humble is a quality of a good man.**

You can kill my body if you want but you will never kill my word.

**My word became your flesh.**

Like a tool my body is. I will get my work done no matter what it takes of me.

**Master the art of silence.**

Resist your urges.

**Everyone's here intentionally.**

Be as good as you can be.

**Wise is he who knows when to mute himself and reserve his speech.**

Sometimes you have to do the wrong thing
for the right reason.

**I don't talk a lot.**

Sometimes it's not so much what you see,
but how you choose to look at things that matters more.

**Just because you could doesn't always mean you should.**

If you establish power, never abuse it.

**Avoid people who try to control other people.**

Don't let other people anger you.

**Be the master of your own temper.**

Sometimes you need to play dumb because not everyone
always has good intentions.

**Some people laugh at your misery.**

Life could be good for everyone but it's not.

**Man's money don't control the seasons.**

Some of your enemies pose as friends.

**You're not me, I'm not you.**

Do what's best for you always.

**Bad exists, but so does good.**

Never be the first one to damage a friendship or bond you have held.

**Pay attention to everything.**

You cannot afford to be ignorant.

**There's an enemy amongst you.**

Time don't stop and the clock is always ticking.

**Be very mindful and very aware of how you spend your time.**

I wish that man loved peace more than he loves war.

**Only carry what you can hold.**

If someone wants war, or they just won't stop until war, destroy them. If someone wants peace give them a hand or a hug.

**Be courageous and brave.**

Do not be afraid of the world.

**Help each other more.**

Every single living thing that has freedom of motion, has an opinion and a personality too. Animals are cool and each have their very own characteristics.

**Good humor is good humor.**

Never be ill minded.

**Everyone does not have the same goals as you. Don't let someone that don't understand what you are trying to do, tell you how to reach your goals.**

My word comes from experience.

**Respect men who paved your path.**

Treat a lady well.

**Care about what people care about.**

Save everything you can.

**There is a very good reason I state everything I state.**

Hell is real but so is Heaven.

**You can't miss something that was never yours.**

Don't get used to bad habits.

**Everyone battles something.**

If you're not giving, you're taking.

**Kill everything that attacks you.**

Think about what you can give.

**What's worth more than friends?**

Let your light shine bright.

**Everything tells me something.**

Avoid corruptive things.

**Nothing God made is stupid.**

Be fast to think but slowly spoken.

**Sadly, if you learn how to place your mistakes on purpose, you're probably good at war.**

Don't bother consuming your own time
trying to understand another man's interpretations.

**There is always a contradiction
because even contradiction has a purpose.**

Focus on Heaven not Hell.

**Don't glorify the wrong things.**

Some people help, some people hurt.
Be somebody that helps.

**Let no one abuse you.**

There's a lot of ways to look at one thing.

**You can learn a lot about someone if you notice what they complain about.**

Some people create confusion on purpose.

**Give until it hurts, and then give some more.**

Don't be over emotional.

**Keep your balance.**

Never let fear be your motive.

**Love is always the same energy.**

The devil gets nervous when you keep doing what's right. He will fight until he can fight no more.

**It is a battle until it is a battle no more.
Have faith and keep going.**

Some people steal your time on purpose. They want to distract you and they want to keep you busy so you don't have time to figure out what they're really doing.

**The Illuminati is not good.
The Illuminati was created by Satan's psychics.
They control the world.**

Be quiet about your goals.

**Succeed in silence.**

Be careful: Some people pretend to be good on purpose because the closer that they get to you and the more that they know about you the more they can hurt you later.

**All people are not good.**

Some people are so evil and they know that they are evil. They hide behind their own faces and fronts.

**Everyone is not like you.**

Some people don't love you the same way that you love them.

**Absorb what's real, avoid fake.**

It's obviously not all good.

**You're all one of God's thoughts.**

Look for more ways to save your money than to spend your money.

**Never abuse someone's kindness.**

Sort your wants and needs,
and only use your money for the right things.

**Teach what is needed to succeed.**

Teach it if they don't know how.

**You are responsible, and will be held accountable for your choices and decisions.**

My mind is a sowing machine.

**What am I doing? Planting seeds.**

Talk about love not hate.

**Don't let how we are different separate us,
let how we are the same unite us.**

Don't let your memory haunt you.

**You are what you continuously do.**

They can't hate you because he loves you.
Look inside yourself.

**Every baby born is love. Hate is a learned behavior that is sadly and unfortunately taught by the world.**

You can't be wrong if you're right.

**The easiest way to pass the time is to sleep.**

Never let another man break you.

**Stay focused on your goal and keep your eye set on your next agenda.**

Satan will use other people's voices and your own thoughts against you.

**Don't text back when you're angry.**

Every life is a story.

**Don't force anything.**

Don't obey the world's clock.

**Live your life on your terms.**

Never corrupt anyone else.

**Some people choose to hurt and corrupt the world, just make sure your name is not involved in that.**

Bless what cursed you.

**The night it falls but the next day it rises.**

Establish the quality of your character.

**Be the good you are.**

You can't stop nature.

**Handle matters with grace.**

Breathe not arrogance.

**Every man must experience death.**

You don't have to accept every thought
that occurs within you.

**Study other things.**

The more you learn the more you know,
and the more you know the more you grow.

**If you are at war learn how to use your enemies' intelligence against him. Deceive his reconnaissance.**

Never tell your enemy the truth.

**There's no honor amongst thieves.**

If you want to be good at war play chess a lot. Learn their responses.

**Ask if your enemy needs a napkin.**

Some people take, and some people give.

**Provoke thoughts, not motions.**

Good is more powerful than bad.

**Right is more powerful than wrong.**

True is more powerful than false.

**Everyone's soul is at war.**

Be conscious about your evolution.

**Only right can win wrong.**

I like love songs.

**Love can reach places hate can't.**

Sometimes fight your own tears.

**If you define yourself, let it be love.
Being hate is a fatal flaw.**

Love is stronger than your worry.

**You are not as old as me.**

I cried and I cried and I cried.

**When an evil man cannot be stopped by your words, he must be stopped by your actions.**

Stop making excuses for other people.
Everyone is not good.

**Sad but true: your enemy will only tell you the truth when you're not paying attention.**

Just because you can does not mean that you should.

**Imagine what I'd be if I listened to everyone that speaks to me.**

Not caring about each other is destroying you all.

**Learn how to play leapfrog.**

I preach two things because there is a contradiction amongst you all.

**Psychics don't exist in Heaven.**

Every parasite needs a true host.

**Have you ever seen a lion yawn?**

Tomorrow will worry about itself.

**Some things are better undefined.**

Stop worrying.

**Spend your time wisely.**

Invest in yourself.

**Confront contradiction.**

If he's angry and you don't know why, just leave him alone. He'll be back when he calms down.

**You need each other a lot.**

Doing what's wrong causes a righteous reaction from God.

**Opinion is a form of judgement.**

Do not let, what is wrong stand within you. It will create friction, contradiction, turbulence, and disturbance.

**Hold onto what is right.**

Life doesn't have to be so hard.

**I hope you're always right.**

You will never conquer my word.

**Strengthen your soul.**

Purify your mind.

**Exercise your body.**

The soul rules the body, but the mind tells the soul
what to do.

**Don't tell the devil your plans.**

If you can quit a bad habit later
you could quit a bad habit now.

**If you could give it a fist you could give it a hand.**

Don't look at each other hatefully.

**Inspire togetherness.**

Try to be in your very own way universal.

**Achieve universal understanding.**

Using your strength for the right reason
is a righteous secret.

**When you love what's right it's easier to stop what's wrong.**

Walk through it all with a smile.

**The right idea will never be wrong.**

If you want to be wise, be right.

**Somehow, someway, someday.**

Shatter the image of hate.

**You are nobody's boss.**

Every man lives his own life.

**The universe will make you learn synergy.
You are together.**

You are responsible for your actions.

**You don't own anything.**

As soon as someone shows you how fake they are,
stay away from them.

**Use their arrogance against them.**

Some people lie on purpose.

**How do you trick a psychic? I don't know.**

Sylvia Browne is in hell.

**Acting stupid is so smart.**

Demons are not gargoyles.

**Suffer now or suffer later.**

Don't gossip a lot.

**Don't accept the devil's suggestions.**

Your enemy is always there.

**Never stop producing your army.**

Expect evil to be in rich places.

**Don't speak bad of your friends.**

Everybody's been through a lot.

**The average man doesn't care about the average man. I think that's sad.**

I hope one day you see and know we're here together and not alone.

**You can learn a lot from silence.**

If you are going through many struggles or troublesome times, you can tackle one thing at a time and conquer them all or you can try to do everything at once and end up get nothing done.

**Fully focus your attention.**

Simulation cannot replace actual experience. Actual experience is a lot more unpredictable than any simulation.

**Live and learn but love and grow.**

Sort your wrongs from rights.

**Learn how to use your enemies' strengths against them.**

Sometimes their motive is money.

**You'll be what you choose to be.**

Avoid ugly thoughts.

**Don't look at each other with evil thoughts.**

Care about others more than you.

**Love what's right, hate what's wrong.**

Feed your brain positive things.

**Let no one tell you that you can't.**

Sometimes impossible things occur beyond understanding.

**You are what you want to be.**

You can't prove to a donkey he's not a horse.

**Use your energy wisely.**

Sometimes life's unbelievable.

**Sad but true: some completely disregard the lives of others.**

You should stay socially and globally conscious.

**All can be good but are not.**

You are what you choose to be.

**One of the nicest things you can say is I understand, but don't say it if you don't mean it.**

Despise an ugly mind.

**Love beautiful thoughts.**

If you want your body to be able to be more powerful, purify your thoughts.

**Don't even look at good things with bad thoughts in your mind.**

Always be good, but train nature
and make life understand you.

**When Satan can see you, he can't hear you, and when he can hear you, he can't see you because he exists in spirit form now and he can only hear your thoughts when he's inside your mind. His spirit's dark. Satan does not have ears or eyes. He sees you by feeling you. The size of his spirit fluctuates but he cannot be outside of you and inside of you at the same time.**

Do now, speak about it later.

**Be humble hearted unless you are forced to rumble.**

A quiet man's voice is loud.

**All you have is a picture.**

You should see it the right way.

**Sleep is necessary but will not strengthen your soul.**

I think every one of you could make this world
a better place.

**You should know that you can only better a worse version of yourself by trying to be the best version of yourself.**

Everyone matters.

**I don't think a man has found himself until he's at least 40.**

I'm clever and wise.

**Stop worrying about people that don't worry about you.**

Talk as little as you can or as much as you need to.

**Sometimes you have to stand alone.**

Be a good person.

**Something will always challenge your goals.**

One problem with this world is that bad rewards you and good does not. The governments need to fix that issue.

**The world is mine, I'll destroy it if I want to.**

Succeed in silence.

**Stop trying to mend bonds you didn't break.**

Pleasure your pain.

**Look at the price of what it costs.**

You remind me.

**Don't complicate your life.**

Enjoy simple things.

**Ignore your eyelashes.**

Avoid being irritable.

**Don't let anyone but you control your emotions and responses.**

You're all one of God's opinions.

**How unwavering is your love?**

Good is good, right is right, and wrong is wrong.

**Care about the right things.**

Plant positive seeds.

**Light can go in dark places.**

Only take what you need.

**Hate is a man-made tendency.**

What you need you can find in each other.

**Try to make every day better than the last.**

The easiest way to stop a bad habit is never to start one.

**We need to teach our children better
so they don't grow into the same problems that we have.**

Shame on they who deceive you, especially for monetary gains.

**Protect your values.**

Establish your virtues.

**At the end of these days, you will have to answer
for what you did, not what they did.**

Keep your path clean.

**Protect your essence.**

If you want the truth about them,
expect it to be a lie sometimes.

**If they lie to you, lie to them.**

Be just so loyal as they are to you.

**Not everyone is worthy of your truth.**

Only an enemy can tame you.

**A friend will understand you.**

Why are contradictions necessary?

**Whatever is right eventually wins.**

Clash with ideas, not with fists.

**Never hate something good.**

Practice being calm.

**Do what you need to do when you need to do it.**

Be careful what you feed the world.

**Invest positive energy.**

You are responsible for you.

**Don't disrespect yourself or others.**

You can't steal a Bible from church.

**Being yourself is not a mistake.**

Pay attention to what they influence within you.

**The more time that you put into something the better it becomes.**

Avoid urges.

**The possibility of good and evil will always exist.**

Check on people who check on you.

**No one's ever too busy.**

What you care about will show.

**Some people think what if we die
but I think what if we live?**

Never put mal-intent in your efforts.

**Know what you need and don't.**

The day will not always be good.

**A lazy man misses his meal.**

Life will test and try you.

**Train your nature.**

There's a difference between what you want to know
and what you need to know.

**Be leery of a man who wants nothing.**

Walk within your purpose.

**Some things don't need to change.**

Some things need to remain the same.

**Every day can be a good day.**

What some people say means almost nothing,
What they do means a lot.

**Build momentum.**

I can see life in your eyes.

**Try to be happy.**

Music influences emotion.

**Don't let the world make you feel like you're not special.**

You can't test a fully taught teacher because he's the one that's testing you.

**Jesus saves.**

Trust God.

This book is dedicated to You.

As well as to my daughter:

Aaliyah Alt

God Bless Your Hearts.

You, Are Love.

www.ingramcontent.com/pod-product-compliance
Lightning Source LLC
LaVergne TN
LVHW021826060526
838201LV00058B/3522